CATS

CATS

Tom Howard

SMITHMARK

First published in the United States in 1992
by SMITHMARK Publishers Inc.,
112 Madison Avenue, New York, NY 10016

in association with Octopus International
a division of Reed International Books Limited

ISBN 0-8317-1203-1

SMITHMARK books are available for bulk purchase for sales
promotion and premium use. For details write or telephone
the Manager of Special Sales, SMITHMARK Publishers Inc.,
112 Madison Avenue, New York, NY 10016. (212) 532-6600.

Printed in Hong Kong

CONTENTS

INTRODUCTION

What is it that makes a cat such a delight to have around? For some people it is the cat's physical grace and beauty, or its obvious intelligence, for others it is its cosy comforting companionship. Psychologists tell us that just stroking a cat's fur can create a sense of calm and relaxation. Cats have great personality and maintain a definite independence. Though often showing a great desire to be involved with people and lavish in their displays of affection, they will disappear about their own business to pursue a lifestyle quite separate from any domestic conditioning.

All these things contribute to the cat's appeal and the cat is rapidly becoming the most popular of household pets. Yet, of all the animals which man has domesticated it is probably the least changed from its natural state. It is only in comparatively recent times that breeders have intervened to produce new breeds and types – a process which has been going on for thousands of years with dogs, horses and other domestic animals. It is not for nothing that the cat has been called 'the tiger on the hearth'.

It is difficult to observe the lives of most mammals, especially the nocturnal hunters, but the cat offers an opportunity for everyone to study the complete life cycle and behaviour of an animal at close quarters in their own homes and backyards. This book draws attention to many aspects of feline life, explaining the behaviour patterns which you can see for yourself if you take the trouble to observe the cats around you.

THE CAT WITH NINE LIVES

Who would think that a cat sitting calmly in the sun or fastidiously washing a paw could live a life of risk and danger? Yet cats have earned a proverbial nine lives from their ability to survive. This is not due to any mystical protection but to a very efficient physique and well-developed senses, although cats can still make mistakes and they have their share of disasters. In some respects their skills outshine those of their owners but there are other areas where their abilities are not so good.

Cats have a very flexible skeleton and good musculature. They can turn their heads, for instance, almost 180° each way, much more than humans. They can produce great spurts of power but because their heart and lungs are comparatively small (more body space is taken up by their digestive system), they cannot sustain activity for long.

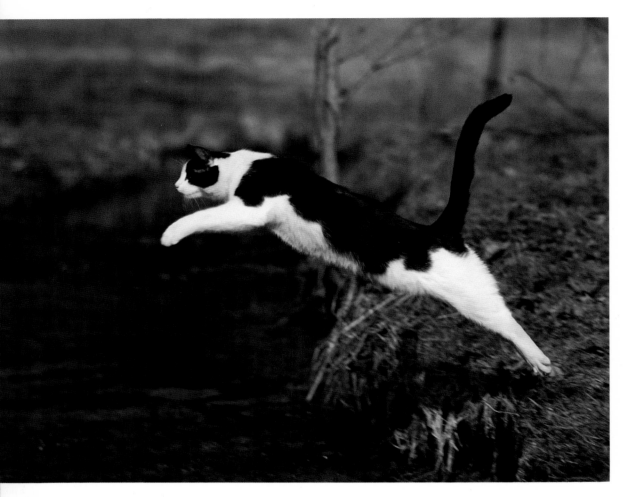

Jumping up on to a wall five times its own height or leaping across a stream offers no problem to the average cat; its powerful hind legs provide tremendous thrust. Jumping downwards it will reduce the height by first stretching down, then trying to push outwards. This gives it more chance of lowering its hind feet during the drop in order to make a four-point landing, and so lessen the impact to be absorbed by each paw.

If they fall from a height, cats are able to turn in the air to align themselves for landing but too forceful an impact can still cause injury, often a fractured palate. Cats falling from heights which enable them to reach maximum velocity before landing are less likely to be injured for, once the speed of fall is steady, they relax, which makes for a softer touchdown.

Cats have an excellent sense of balance; this involves structures within the inner ear known as the 'vestibular apparatus', which used to be thought somehow different from ours – but tightrope walkers develop similar skills. Although cats use their tails in balance control, Manx and other tailless cats do not seem to be handicapped.

Cats have good spatial sense, squeezing through small holes and rarely bumping into things. It is often thought that their whiskers grow to the width of their bodies and act as a measure of whether they can get through spaces. Whiskers certainly play a part for, together with similar hairs on the backs of the front paws, they are sensitive to air pressure which subtly changes according to the position of surrounding objects.

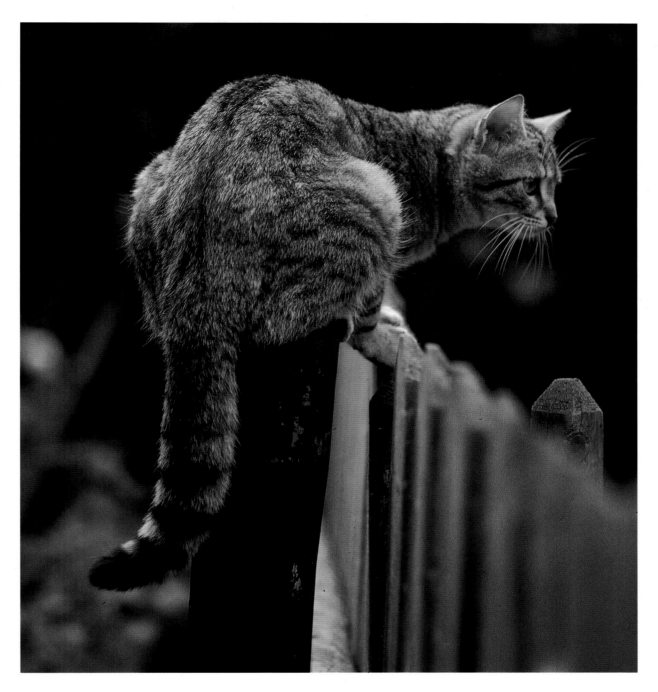

Watch a cat's ears prick up when it hears something of interest; they are extremely flexible and can turn a full half circle in the direction of the sound. Cats' sharp hearing is not so effective as our own in the lower ranges but extends much higher, well into the range of bats' sonic squeaks. Cats learn to ignore all kinds of general noises but react instantly to any sounds which have a relevance to their lives. Out of the general murmur of traffic they will recognize the family car's engine or identify the footsteps of a friend long before they reach the house. Being able to hear and locate the slightest rustle in the undergrowth or barnyard straw is a great asset to the hunter.

Smell is of immense importance to a cat. It carries vital information about food, about dangers, about sex and about territory. This ginger and white cat smelling a twig has registered that it has been sprayed by a dog and has slightly raised its tail fur, a reaction to a potential threat.

The membrane sensitive to smell in the cat's nose covers nearly twice the area it does in humans, and cats also have an additional scent organ between nose and palate, known as Jacobson's organ. You will often see a cat sitting with its mouth slightly open in an expression of apparent disdain – known by scientists as the 'flehmen' reaction. The cat is actually sucking in scent particles and transferring them from its tongue to channels behind the upper teeth which connect with this scent organ.

Cats can't really see in the dark, they must rely upon their other senses, but their eyes are adapted to make full use of any available light however dim. In bright light the pupils of their eyes narrow to a tiny slit, preventing dazzle; as it gets dark they open wide to admit as much as possible. A surface at the back of the eye then reflects light forward, enabling it to use that light twice over. It is this that makes a cat's eyes appear to shine in the dark.

Humans have a sharper focus and much better colour vision than the cat but these are not much use in dim light and the cat's eyes are much better adapted to the world of the night hunter.

Like all mammals, cats are warm blooded. Except when tiny kittens, or under very extreme conditions, they are able to maintain their body temperature at an even level and be active at all times, unlike reptiles which must wait for the sun to warm them up. Their furry coat provides insulation against heat loss.

The types of cat which were first domesticated had short fur, and longhaired cats, especially those which have been selectively bred to have very luxuriant coats, are not always able to take care of them on their own. Show cats need a lot of grooming and even domestic pets should have a daily brushing.

When parents are of a different coat type or colour short fur is always dominant over long, and tabby over single colours and other patterns. Red colour is caused by a gene carried on the pair of chromosomes which determine sex and though a male can inherit the red colouring it is theoretically not possible for it to inherit the combination of genes to produce a tortoiseshell coat of red, black and cream; although the occasional male tortoiseshell appears, due to a rare chromosome imbalance, such cats are nearly always sterile.

From parents' pedigrees breeders can predict the colour and body type of kittens. Once a particular type exists carefully selected matings can produce a whole range of colours.

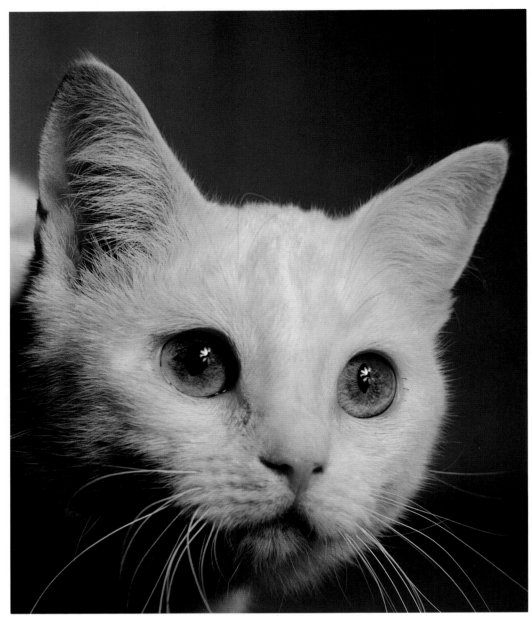

The Chinchilla (right) is one of the most beautiful of cats. Its long, silky white fur is tipped with black, giving the coat a sparkling appearance. The brick red nose and the blue-green or emerald eyes are outlined in black adding to its dazzling appearance.

Eye colour is inherited independently of coat colour but blue eyes when linked with white fur are associated with deafness in cats. Kittens born with even the smallest area of coloured fur, even though it disappears when they mature, are not genetically white, and so are unaffected, but odd-eyed white cats, as above, are sometimes deaf in just one ear.

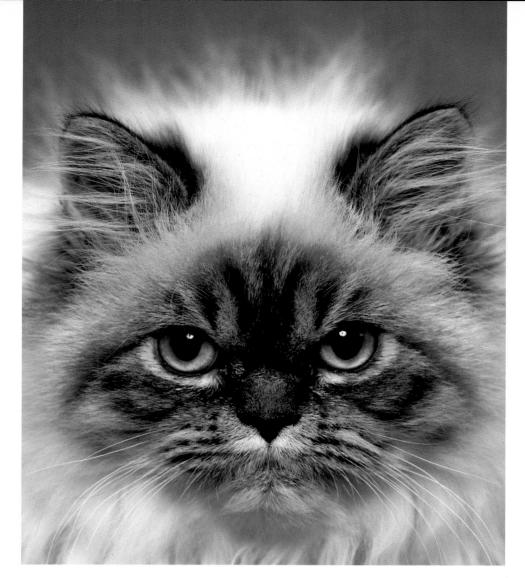

When people first began to exhibit cats competitively it was the long-haired Persian cats which attracted most attention with their luxuriant fur. Pale coats with colour restricted to the face, tail and limbs – a 'pointed' pattern like that of the Siamese, were a much later development and some people classify them as a different breed, the Colourpoints (left and above). Long furred or short, sleek and elegant or short and stocky, blue-blooded pedigree or alley cat, each animal has its own individual character. Personality can vary more between cat and cat than can be categorized as particular to a breed. Yet, different though each may be, all share those instincts, skills and behaviour patterns which mark them out as distinctively cats.

CAT BEHAVIOUR

The cat has evolved as an efficient predator but however perfect its hunter's physique it will starve if it has no prey to catch. It must establish a hunting territory and, within that, a core territory which is likely to be rigorously defended. Territory size will reflect both prey supply and the pressure of feline numbers. Even domestic cats, which have no need to hunt for food, have a strong sense of territory.

A newcomer has to find its own patch, perhaps driving out a cat already claiming its back yard. Territorial boundaries can be very complex. A cat may not have claim to the roof it lives beneath and a garden may be divided between several cats, none of whom live in the house to which it belongs.

A cat marks its territory at various points, not necessarily its perimeter, by spraying urine, by scratching, which leaves a scent mark from the paw pads as well as the visible signs, and by rubbing its body against objects, bringing scent secreting glands on the temples, chin and base of the tail into contact.

Marking is not necessarily a signal to keep out, more of a calling card. Cats will investigate a point marked by another cat with interest not fear. Although territory will be defended against a cat who tries to take it over there is rarely any attempt to prevent another passing through and often, especially in urban areas, there will be areas which are shared.

Cats usually avoid confrontation and only fight as a last resort. They go through a series of preliminary manoeuvres to try to resolve the situation without actually coming to blows. After an exchange of threats and posturings one will usually acknowledge the other's superiority, indicating submission by making itself seem as small as possible, often crouching low with ears flattened forwards.

The familiar arched back and fluffed-up fur is created by a combination of reactions as fear encourages the cat to retreat and bravado tells it to advance. Almost all confrontations show a mixture of threatening and defensive response.

Cats evolved as nocturnal hunters, being most efficient in the half light of dusk and early morning. The domestic pet retains its hunting instincts and will chase and catch, but unless introduced to live prey by its mother, a kitten will not necessarily connect hunting for prey with food.

Cats have two main hunting techniques: stalking and ambush. A cat will wait patiently next to a mouse hole or beside a route along which prey is known to pass, ready to pounce when a suitable victim appears. Experienced cats will not spring on a mouse the moment it emerges from a hole – it might be able to bolt back inside again. They wait until it has come too far to dive back to safety.

Seen almost in monochrome by prey animals, most cats are very well camouflaged among grasses and undergrowth but they make themselves even less noticeable by keeping their bodies close to the ground. Moving quickly through thick cover or crossing open ground they approach very stealthily when they think prey are near, getting as close as possible before making the final attack and freezing mid-movement if there is any risk they have been spotted.

A cat watching a bird that is out of reach or through a window often makes a chattering, staccato sound. Why, is a mystery. Is it excitement or a sign of irritation, a challenge or a threat?

Sleep accounts for up to two-thirds of a cat's life. Wild cats are active at night but domestic pets, especially if allowed to sleep on their owner's bed, often adapt themselves to human life patterns. They may not sleep the whole night in a single stretch and will still often sleep during the day, especially if their people are out. The normal sleep pattern consists of many shortish periods. Much of the time this is shallow sleep, when the cat can register external stimuli and respond to danger. For periods of six or seven minutes this can become deep sleep when the cat is completely relaxed. It is then a cat may dream – but the twitching of paws and whiskers does not mean it is pursuing a dream hunt. It is merely a discharge of surplus electrical energy in the muscles.

THE CAT'S DAY

Adult cats do not waste energy. In the wild, strenuous effort is reserved for hunting and other necessary activity. Cats will have a main sleeping place at the heart of their core territory – curled up on their owner's bed for many domestic pets – but will catnap in all kinds of unlikely places, often having a succession of spots to fit different conditions or times of day.

They like fixed hours for meals, play sessions, grooming and being let out to socialize and hunt (and being let in again), all matched to a regular routine. They have a good sense of time and will probably let you know if you do not keep to the schedule.

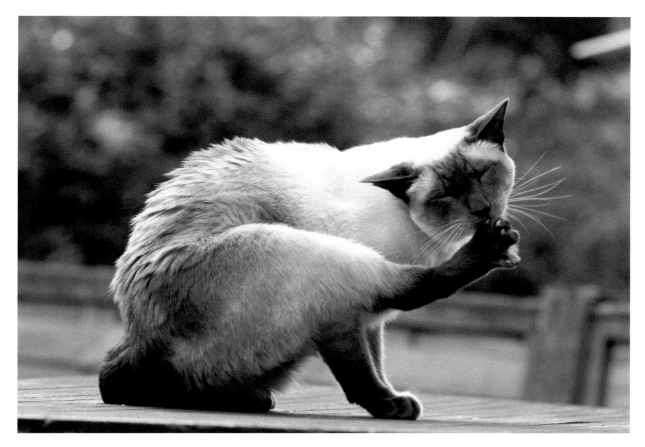

The first activity on waking is usually a good stretch followed by a wash – unless it has been a long sleep and a toilet call is needed. 'If in doubt, wash' seems to be the cats' catechism. Cats are always washing – partly because they like to be clean, partly as a displacement activity to hide embarrassment, give them time to think, distract attention from their real intentions, or pretend that they are just not interested. A cat's tongue is covered with backward pointing sharp papillae which form a rasp, ideal for scraping flesh off bones and an efficient washcloth and hairbrush. Where the tongue cannot reach cats clean with a tongue-moistened paw. Washing is also a way to keep cool in hot weather, evaporation of saliva from the fur helps to reduce their temperature.

Cats find it very satisfying to dig their claws into a piece of wood or furniture and have a good stretch. This is quite different from deliberate scratching, which is used as a marker. Another form of scratching 'sharpens' the claws – not really sharpening but removing the blunted outer layer to reveal a sharp new tip. Cats usually have a favourite place for this activity – which may also be scratch marked. If it is a piece of furniture it can be very badly damaged. Luckily cats are easily trained to use a log or a piece of coarse cloth mounted on a stand or against the wall. Notice whether your cat prefers to perform this action on the floor or against a vertical before deciding what to offer for its use.

Cats have always got an eye and ear open for a friend, even a stranger well-disposed to cats, who can be cajoled into giving them some attention. A roll upon the ground with the belly exposed is a bold declaration that a cat wants to be friends and an invitation to play or pet.

Some cats like to have their exposed tummy tickled but beware, not all find this acceptable and the presentation of the underparts, which to another cat is a clear indication of submission by offering the most vulnerable body area, also brings into play a pair of powerful weapons – the hind legs and their claws. A cat that does not like being tickled may defend itself by giving you a raking slash.

All kittens play games, it is part of the learning process. Since one of the effects of domestication is to preserve some infantile characteristics, including play, the adult pet has a much stronger tendency to play than do wild feline species. Play behaviour will be especially strong where it is maintained by regular games with human companions. It may range from chasing string to football, retrieving and hide-and-seek. A game with a partner, animal or human, is usually preferred, but lots of cats will also play on their own.

B ack home again, a good scratch to get the
circulation going and dislodge any bits
picked up on the fur, is followed by
another wash. Then cats will usually circle a few
times on the spot, an instinctive move to settle a
nest out in the wild, and time for another nap –
in front of a nice warm fire if possible. Cats
really enjoy lying in the sun, on top of a boiler
or near a radiator or an open fire. They often get
so close that they singe their fur and can even
have their tail right in a flame before they
register the heat.

When confident and warm a cat will stretch its
body wide, both to enjoy the heat and because
there is no need to conserve it. In cold
conditions a cat will curl up and surround itself
with an insulating ball of fur, its tail tip probably
covering its nose.

FAMILY LIFE

Cats usually make excellent mothers and most give birth with no problems whatsoever, although they have their share of breech births, stillbirths and Caesarians. The problem is not having kittens but how to find them homes. Although cats are now such popular pets there are still a great many unwanted kittens born and animal welfare organizations have to destroy thousands and thousands of cats and kittens every year. For the owner who is confident that homes are waiting for his or her cat's kittens there is nothing more delightful than seeing and sharing in the raising of a litter but otherwise spaying of females and neutering of all pet toms is the only way of ensuring that unwanted kittens are not born.

E xploring the world is not all plain sailing. Things are not always as easy as they look. Having discovered how easy it is to climb up a tree a kitten then has to face the problem of getting down again and discovers that that requires a different technique. Many things a kitten must learn for itself, and the process will go on long after it has grown up.

Dealing with other animals is another area in which a kitten gains experience. Fortunately many animals show a general tolerance of the young even of other species and though a kitten may go through the whole range of confrontational postures they will not be provoked. If the kitten is not so lucky its tree-climbing technique could come in useful.

At eight weeks old a kitten should have a full set of teeth teeth and be fully weaned on to solid food, although that does not mean that it will not attempt to suckle if it sees the opportunity. By this time, many cat mothers probably find the kittens' teeth are making their nipples sore and are becoming irritated by constant demands for milk, even though they are still producing it. The kittens have now developed considerable independence, although there are still many things they can learn from their mother and from interaction with brothers and sisters. Domestic pets should not leave for their new homes until they are twelve weeks old; in the wild the family would stay together much longer before going off to establish their own territories.

Feral cats become efficient scavengers, adept at spotting spilled milk and begging at tourist pavement restaurants as well as raiding garbage cans but *every* cat is an opportunist. Even the best-cared-for pet seems convinced that someone else's dinner must taste better than its own and that stolen food has a much better flavour. To leave food out unattended is asking for trouble even though a cat may seem a perfect angel when you are watching it. Puss knows that by the time he's climbed up to the bird table the prey will all have flown but it is their food, and not the birds, he's after.

As naturalist Gilbert White observed, it is strange that cats, which usually have a distaste for getting wet, so enjoy a fishy diet. They will often watch fish swimming in a pond or stream for hours and some manage to become adept at putting in a paw and flipping them out. There are even authenticated cases – though only one or two – of cats which habitually dived in and brought fish out.

A cat which accidentally finds itself in the water will usually instinctively swim with a dog-paddle fore-paw action but they do not have the stamina to keep going for long.

Lucky the quayside cat who gets fresh fish each morning. It *may* be patient – it will get its own share soon – but cats find it very difficult to resist temptation!

ACKNOWLEDGEMENTS

Animal Photography/Sally Anne Thompson 20, 24, 80-1, 90-1; Animals Unlimited 1, 32, 72-3; Ardea 78, 80; Bruce Coleman/Jim Bain 43; Bruce Coleman/Jane Burton 2, 18-19, 27, 41, 53, 54-55, 58, 59, 66-7, 67, 69, 74-5, 82-3, 84, 85; Bruce Coleman/Jane Burton and Kim Taylor 10-11, 20-1; Bruce Coleman/Eric Crichton 5; Bruce Coleman/Hans Reinhard 6, 16, 22-3, 34-5, 37, 39, 46-7, 60-1, 68-9; Sally and Richard Greenhill 48, 93; Natural History Photographic Agency/Henry Ausloos 64-5; Stephen Dalton 76, 77; Octopus Publishing Group Ltd/Peter Loughran 29/John Moss 28, 32-3; Solitaire Photographic 26, 88, 88-9; Spectrum Colour Library 8-9, 12, 13, 14-15, 30-1, 42-3, 46, 49, 50-1, 56-7, 57, 62-3, 73, 92, 94-5; Zefa Picture Library 10, 17, 25, 36, 38, 40, 44-5, 52, 70-1, 74, 79, 86-7.